9·07

FACE TO FACE WITH
DOLPHINS

by Flip and Linda Nicklin

NATIONAL GEOGRAPHIC
WASHINGTON, D.C.

FACE TO FACE

I have been an underwater photographer for many years. I have been lucky to have the chance to swim with many different kinds of sea creatures. My specialty is whales and dolphins.

One day, I went out on a boat with a group of researchers. I could tell from the start that this day was going to be special.

We were anchored in a shallow area 40 miles off the coast of the Bahamas. The researchers would travel by boat to this spot and wait for

← *An Atlantic spotted dolphin named Romeo takes a closer look.*

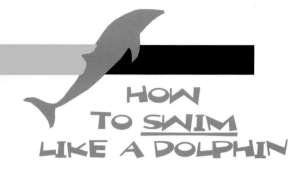

HOW TO SWIM LIKE A DOLPHIN

— Find a pool or some other place where it is safe to swim.

— Put on fins, mask, and snorkel.

— Get in the water and lie face down.

— Breathe out of your "blowhole," the snorkel that sticks out of the water past the back of your head.

— Keep your feet together and move them up and down, like the tail of a dolphin.

— Tuck your upper arms in by your sides so you will be streamlined.

— Stick your lower arms and hands out to be side fins. Hold them so they make you more stable as you move through the water.

— Keep those powerful feet kicking together like dolphin tails!

wild dolphins to come by, so they could study their behavior. Sometimes we stayed for weeks, watching them every chance we could.

One day, a group of Atlantic spotted dolphins approached. I pulled on my fins, mask, and snorkel, picked up my camera in its special underwater case, and slipped over the side of the boat. Dolphins swim very fast. That makes it hard to take pictures of them or to observe their behavior underwater. But sometimes the dolphins swim slowly. They let us watch them interacting with each other. These dolphins did that.

The researchers could identify one dolphin in the group by its markings. They had even given him a name: Romeo. Romeo was a playful dolphin. That day he played with me by making me spin like a top. First, he came up very close. All I could see through the camera was his face. He looked me right in the eye. Then he swam slowly around me. I had to keep turning to keep his face in the lens. Once he had me spinning, he swam faster and faster. I got dizzy trying to keep up with him. When I stopped, he went off to play with someone else.

A dusky dolphin near South Island in New Zealand. These guys can really leap!

Whales and dolphins are the ones in charge when I photograph them. I am slow and awkward in the water compared to these powerful swimmers, and they can always swim away. With Romeo, it was obvious that we were playing the game he wanted to play. And that day I saw something I've noticed many times since: Dolphins are good at finding ways to have fun.

MEET

An Amazon River dolphin in the shallow water of a lake called Lago de Prata in Brazil. This dolphin is used to being fed by people, so it quickly came in close.

THE DOLPHIN

Four bottlenose dolphins at Ocean Quest Hawaii investigate me as I hold my breath and take their picture.

When I first picked up a camera, I never thought that one day I would be standing in a lake in Brazil with a long-snouted dolphin nibbling playfully at my ankles. But that is just what happened.

Dolphins live in all the oceans on the planet. Some of them even live in rivers. There are many kinds, or species, of dolphin. The dolphin that was playfully nibbling at my ankles like a frisky puppy that day was an Amazon River dolphin. It is one of five species that live in fresh water.

↑ 1 Bottlenose dolphins can grow to 12 feet (4 meters) long. Males can weigh 1,100 pounds (500 kilograms). They live world-wide in oceans and as captive dolphins in aquariums. 2 A dusky dolphin leaps near Kaikura, New Zealand. 3 Orcas' diets include fish, seals, otters, and even deer. 4 Tucuxi, a freshwater species found in Brazil. 5 Hawaiian spinner dolphins rotate as they leap. 6 Common dolphins can be seen in groups of thousands.

If you have seen a dolphin on television or at an aquarium, it was probably a bottlenose dolphin, one of 33 marine, or ocean, species. The smallest dolphin species grows to less than five feet (two meters) long. The biggest dolphin gets so big we call it a whale: The orca, or killer whale, can be over 29 feet (9 meters) long.

The different kinds of dolphins are alike in many ways. They are not fish. They are mammals, like us. Like all mammals, dolphins breathe air. To do this, they come to the surface of the water. They breathe through a special opening on their heads called a blowhole. When dolphins are relaxed or underwater, their blowholes are closed. As you can imagine, this makes it tricky for them to sleep. Instead of sleeping

all night like we do, they rest for short periods. They stay still and quiet underwater, then come to the surface when they need to take a breath.

Most dolphins can see well, though some of the river dolphins that live in cloudy water have poor eyesight. But even in clear water, it is hard to see very far. So dolphins have a super-sense that helps them hunt and find their way around their watery world. We call this sense "echolocation."

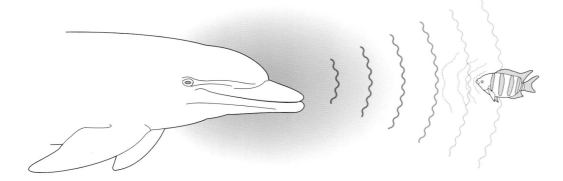

Dolphins use sound to tell them where things are. They send out sounds that bounce off things around them. When the sounds come back, the dolphin "hears" what's around it. The sound bounces off objects like light bounces off things when you shine a flashlight on them. This sound-sensing is called echolocation. Using sound, dolphins can sense even small details underwater. They can tell what kinds of fish are nearby. They know what direction the fish are swimming and how fast— even in the dark.

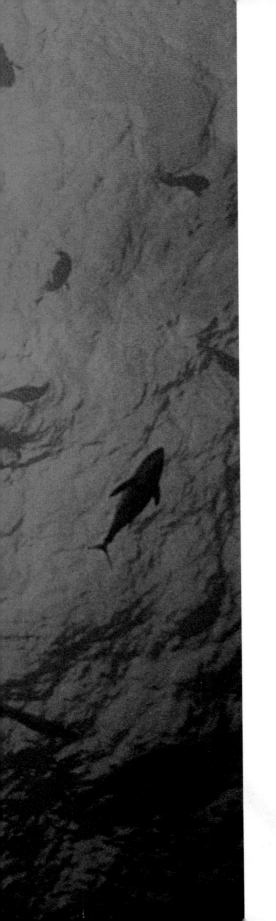

Bottlenose dolphins feed on fish that have schooled under a floating log near Cocos Island, Costa Rica. (I'm looking up from below.) Also in the picture are tuna and birds feeding on the same "bait ball."

1 Young Atlantic spotted dolphins swim playfully with each other. 2 A dolphin baby stays close to its mother and nurses on her rich milk. Later on, she will teach it to catch fish.

Dolphins swim all the time, and they are very good at it. The fastest of them can swim faster than 20 miles (32 kilometers) per hour. Some dolphins can leap high out of the water. Many like to ride waves near ocean beaches or the bows of boats. Most can dive deep. All dolphins can hold their breath much longer than we can. Their strength and keen senses help them catch food. What's on the menu if you are a dolphin? Fish, squid, lobsters, shrimp, and crabs.

This orca at SeaWorld San Diego has helped people get familiar with its kind. Here it shows its teeth and makes sounds for the audience.

FAMILY LIFE

A mature male orca, with its straight six-foot-tall (two-meter) dorsal fin, swims with other members of its pod, or family. Some orcas stay with their mothers for their whole life, so one pod might include a grandmother and her children and grandchildren.

Dolphins have one baby at a time. Youngsters stay close to their mothers in the first months of life, learning from them. I once watched a baby orca in Alaska swimming with its mother. The mother was teaching the baby how to catch fish. She chased a salmon, a kind of fish, just enough to keep it close. Then the baby orca would try to catch it.

Most dolphins live in groups, so we call them "social" animals. Each member of the group helps the others. Some might keep a lookout for danger

➡ *A playful one-year-old orca researchers call Arriga leaps while swimming with his family in Alaska. Different families sometimes socialize.*

⬇ *These Atlantic spotted dolphins can spend their whole lives with family members or other dolphins in their group. They help each other, learn from each other, and play together.*

A group of Hawaiian spinner dolphins rest in a shallow sandy area near Lanai, Hawaii.

while others rest. One can alert another of nearby food. Dolphins even hunt cooperatively. They swim side-by-side in a line to herd fish, or they make a circle so that fish pack together and are easier to catch. If a dolphin is hurt, others may protect it.

People who study dolphins can identify individual animals by the shape of their fins and their markings. We have learned more about dolphins by watching one animal over time, even if we don't see it every day. By studying individuals, we learned that dolphin families tend to stay together. We also found that dolphins living on one side of the world may not have the same habits and ways of life as dolphins in another area, even when they are of the same species. They make different sounds and prefer different foods, just like people in England do some things differently from people in Brazil.

HOW TO SPEAK DOLPHIN

- Dolphins make sounds like whistles, barks, or clicks to communicate with each other or locate things around them.

- Some dolphins have a certain sound that identifies them as individuals. Instead of saying your name, you could identify yourself by whistling in a special way.

- Listen to dolphins on a tape or video. Then blow up a balloon and hold the neck of it. Can you make a sound like a dolphin by stretching the neck and letting the air out slowly?

PEOPLE

Swimming with a dolphin can be fun and exciting.

& DOLPHINS

Some parks and aquariums allow dolphins and people to interact.

In my career as a photographer, I have been very fortunate. I get to work with some of the scientists who are finding out about dolphins. Their work is important because the more we know about dolphins, the more we can be good neighbors sharing Planet Earth with them. We must understand their behaviors and their needs. Then we can make decisions about our use of the oceans—decisions that will be good for both humans and dolphins.

Human activities affect dolphins in lots of ways. In some places, people hunt dolphins for food, and sometimes too many are killed in one area. But dolphins face even bigger threats from fisheries that spread large nets for shrimp, swordfish, and other seafood. Dolphins accidentally get tangled in the nets and drown. This was a big problem with tuna

fisheries. People protested, and laws were passed to protect the dolphins. Better fishing methods were created that let dolphins escape the nets. In the grocery store, look for cans of tuna that say "dolphin safe." This means the tuna comes from a fishery that uses these methods to avoid killing dolphins.

Pollution and global warming can affect dolphins, too. If the ocean gets warmer in a certain area, the fish that live there might not be able to survive. If the fish die, the dolphins

A park ranger introduces visitors to a wild bottlenose dolphin in Shark Bay, Australia. This animal comes voluntarily to be with people, making it an ambassador for its kind.

HOW DOLPHINS PLAY

- **With water:** riding on bow waves of boats or body-surfing on ocean waves

- **With other species:** sliding off the noses of big whales; "teasing" eels to get them to come out of their holes or puffer fish to get them to inflate; imitating other sea creatures

- **With objects they find:** playing catch or chase with a stick or piece of plastic; draping themselves with seaweed

- **With each other:** chasing games; acrobatic swimming; cuddling

might have trouble finding enough food. Pollution can also kill the food they depend on. Fish that have been poisoned by chemicals can make dolphins sick. And noise from boats sometimes interferes with the dolphin's ability to communicate or echolocate. That's why it is important to understand what dolphins need and how to keep the oceans healthy for all.

Dolphins affect people as well. They can adapt to human companionship and can be taught to perform tasks or play games. They are good imitators, and they like new things. Dolphins are fast, strong, curious, and clever. They even look like they are smiling, although that is just the way their faces are shaped.

These traits make it easy for people all over the world to love dolphins. When we see a dolphin at

➡ *Human activities have a big impact on some of the places dolphins live. These dolphins swim among oil refineries and fishing boats off the coast of Texas.*

← *This captive bottlenose dolphin playing with a plastic six-pack holder shows how trash in the water can be a real danger to wild animals.*

A dolphin at sunset is an inspiring sight.

an aquarium or in the ocean, we often feel delight. They make us feel more curious about animals in general, especially when they look at us as if they are interested in us, too. Dolphins are playful, lively ambassadors. They help us care about the ocean world we share. They help us realize that what is good for dolphins is good for people.

When those dolphins in the Bahamas slowed down to stay around me while I swam, I felt like I was part of their group for a little while. I was the slow, quiet guy, but still, they were choosing to be with me. It made me realize that there is still a lot we don't know about these smart, social animals. And watching them swim, I thought: It is going to be really fun to find out the rest of the story.

HOW YOU CAN HELP

↑ *Children study an orca in captivity at SeaWorld. The orca seems to study the children, too.*

■ The health of our land, streams, and oceans is connected. Almost all of the water that falls as rain or runs in a stream or river eventually ends up in the ocean.

■ Find out about the water that comes out of the faucets in your home. Where does it come from? Where does it go?

■ Sometimes water gets polluted. Chemicals that we put on the lawn can end up in our rivers. Don't throw toxic things like some paints, motor oil, and batteries down drains or in the garbage. Learn what to do with harmful household waste so it does not end up in sewage treatment plants or landfills. Sometimes cities or towns will have a place where you can bring it. Recycle aluminum, glass, and newspapers. Reuse plastic bags.

■ Some waterways have a lot of trash near them. You could help a scouting, 4-H, or school environmental club clean up a stream or other area. You and your group could even adopt a nearby stream. You can get more information from Adopt-a-Stream (www.adopt-a-stream.org) or the Adopt-a-Stream Foundation (www.stream keeper.org).

■ When you visit the beach, be careful not to leave garbage behind. Plastic things can be deadly to animals. Ask your parents to help you pick up any nylon fishing lines or plastic six-pack holders that you see. Your family or group could also help with the International Coastal Cleanup. It is sponsored by the Center for Marine Conservation and takes place on the third Saturday of every September.

■ Ask your parents only to buy tuna fish that has "dolphin safe" on the label.

■ Kids for Saving Earth offers more good ideas for how you can help (http://www.kidsforsavingearth.org).

IT'S YOUR TURN

1 Aquariums and marine parks in Florida, California, Hawaii, and other places have glass-sided tanks to let you watch dolphins swimming and playing underwater. You may be able to feed them and stroke their wet, slippery heads. There may be a pool theater, where trainers show you how high dolphins leap, how fast they swim, and how smart they are.

▼ An orca can jump so its snout is 40 feet (12 meters) out of the water.

2 Would you like to take your own pictures of dolphins? Here are some ideas to get you started. Let the camera see as you do when you watch the animals. Pick out a dolphin that interests you. Maybe it's the smallest, the biggest, or the friendliest. Does it have any marking that identifies it, like a fin with a cut or scar? An unusual pattern on its skin? Take a picture of that. Photograph your dolphin as it swims at a distance, then when it comes close. You may be able to get a close-up of the shiny skin or the pointed teeth when the mouth opens for a fish! Try to get photos of the animal at rest, then swimming fast. A video camera is great for this.

3 You can sometimes spot wild dolphins from beaches on both the Atlantic and Pacific coasts. They may be far out in the water, though. See if you can follow them using a pair of binoculars. Boat tours for watching wild dolphins and whales can take you up close. You can see them moving free in their own habitats. You could videotape the dolphins "bow riding" or leaping. Be sure to respect the animals. Keep your distance when you take pictures.

FACTS AT A GLANCE

⬆ *Three bottlenose dolphins slow down and swim close together to stay in front of our boat.*

Types of dolphins

There are five species of river dolphins. Three of these live only in rivers. All are less than 10 feet (3 meters) long and weigh less than 400 pounds (181 kilograms). There are 33 species of dolphins that live in the seas and oceans. The largest (orca) can be 30 feet (9 meters) long and weigh 12,000 pounds (5,443 kilograms). The smallest may be only 6 feet (2 meters) long and weigh less than 150 pounds (68 kilograms).

Colors are mainly dark gray or black and white in various patterns. River dolphins include pinkish individuals.

Lifespans

Orcas sometimes live 80 to 90 years. Small dolphins live about 15 years.

Food

All dolphins eat fish. Some like shrimp and squid. River dolphins will eat small shellfish and turtles. Many species hunt in groups, herding schools of fish. Orcas eat sharks, salmon, seals, otters, and small whales. Orcas even prey on moose and deer, catching them when they swim across saltwater inlets.

Habitat

Most dolphin species live in salt water in the temperate and tropical zones. Some stay close to coastlines. Others live far out in the ocean. Some dolphin species migrate between these areas. River dolphins live in the Amazon, Irrawaddy, Ganges, Indus, and Yangtze Rivers.

Behavior

Every dolphin species behaves a little differently from every other. Some dolphins live together in groups of 100 or more; others swim with only five or ten companions or family members. There are species that join in masses of 1,000 dolphins for a short time. Orcas may form large groups of many families. They travel, hunt, and play together for years. Amazon River dolphins live alone.

Like whales, dolphins "breach," leaping high out of the water. Spinner dolphins twirl and twist as they leap. Dolphins also "spyhop," lifting just their heads out of water to look around. Commerson's dolphins are high-speed swimmers. They surf the tops of the waves, swim upside-down, and ride on the bow waves of fast boats.

Dolphins are known to help other dolphins of their group who are sick or injured. There are even stories of dolphins protecting humans from shark attacks or helping drowning humans get to land.

Reproduction

Most male and female dolphin pairs do not stay together. A single baby, called a calf, is born to each mother about once every two to five years, depending on the species. Calves drink their mothers' milk and begin to eat fish after a few months. They stay with their mothers for a long while. Some mothers and babies remain close their whole lives.

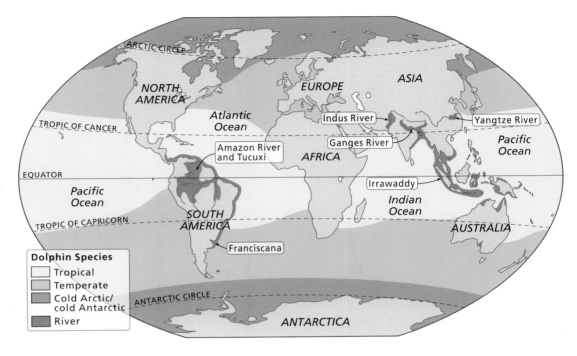

Special features

Big brains and different ways to communicate are dolphin specialties. Dolphins use whistles, squeaks, chirps, clicks, and other noises to talk to each other. They hunt by bouncing sound waves off their prey, like bats do. They also use this "sonar" to stun fish.

Biggest threats

Several dolphin species are in danger. The Yangtze River

⬆ *Dolphins live in all the oceans. River species are identified in rectangles here.*

dolphin may soon become extinct. Fishing nets trap and kill thousands of dolphins every year. And as growing human populations seek to catch more fish, there are fewer left for the dolphins. Pollution is a threat, too. Global warming is changing the dolphins' environment.

29

GLOSSARY

Aquarium A park or attraction that specializes in animals and plants that live in water. Also known as a seaquarium or oceanarium.

Blowhole A breathing hole on the top of dolphins' heads. Like a nose, it takes air in and lets it out.

Bow wave Wave created in front of a moving boat.

Fishery A company or group of fishermen whose business is fishing. Fisheries may use large ships and spread nets across miles of ocean.

Global warming A gradual rise in average temperatures worldwide.

Mammal Air-breathing, warm-blooded animals with hair whose offspring nurse on their mother's milk.

Marine mammal A mammal that lives in or is dependent on the sea or ocean. A dolphin is a marine mammal.

Pollution Waste, garbage, and other undesirable things that dirty water, air, or land.

Porpoise A marine mammal closely related to dolphins. Porpoises have flat-topped teeth and rounded noses, and are smaller than most dolphins.

Research Scientific investigation about a topic; an attempt to answer a question by looking at evidence.

Snorkel A tube that people use to breathe through when they swim. It is usually used with a mask.

Species A group of animals or plants that looks similar, that can breed with each other, and whose offspring can also breed successfully.

FIND OUT MORE

Books & Articles

Berger, Melvin and Gilda. *Do Whales Have Belly Buttons?* New York: Scholastic Reference, 1999.

Carwardine, Mark, Erich Hoyt, R. Ewan Fordyce, Peter Gill. *Whales, Dolphins & Porpoises.* Alexandria, VA: Time-Life Books, 1998.

Dudzinski, Kathleen. *Meeting Dolphins: My Adventures in the Sea.* Washington, D.C.: National Geographic Society, 2000.

Mead, James G., Joy P. Gold, Flip Nicklin. *Whales and Dolphins in Question.* Washington, D.C.: Smithsonian Institution, 2002.

Montgomery, Sy. *Encantado: Pink Dolphin of the Amazon.* Boston: Houghton Mifflin Company, 2002.

Pfeffer, Wendy. *Dolphin Talk: Whistles, Clicks, and Clapping Jaws.* New York: HarperCollins, 2003.

Web Sites

http://www.nationalgeographic.com/kids/creature_feature/0108/dolphins.html
http://thedolphinplace.com

http://dolphins.tappedinto.com
The Wild Dolphin Project studies Atlantic spotted dolphins, including Romeo.
http://www.sandiegozoo.org/animal bytes/t-dolphin.html

http://www.sarasotadolphin.org
Click "Dolphins in Depth" for activities to help you learn more about dolphins.

www.wdcs.org *This site includes games and lots of information.*

www.defenders.org *Search "dolphin"*

www.vanaqua.org *The Vancouver Aquarium, B.C., Canada*

INDEX

RESEARCH & PHOTOGRAPHIC NOTES

Dolphins are a challenge to photograph. To take good pictures of them, I need to know where they live and what they do. I often need to know about their individual personalities. To get these pictures, I worked with a number of researchers and dolphin experts who were willing to share their knowledge with me and help me.

Many of these pictures come from working with researchers "in the field"— usually on a boat on the ocean. Others were taken in an artificial lagoon in Hawaii. I am careful about whom I work with. I am concerned about the health and safety of the dolphins. I don't chase them to get a picture.

There is nothing more important than time and patience in the photography of animals. I can go for weeks without taking a useable picture, waiting for the right situation, light, and timing to all come together. After the long wait, I might get all I hoped for in a few minutes.

I try to keep my gear simple so I can be ready for things to happen and not take up too much room on a small boat. I use an underwater case for an SLR digital camera now, but most pictures in this book were taken with 35mm film. Underwater I use very wide lenses, since I have to be close to get a clear picture. Above water I use medium telephoto lenses and shoot at high shutter speeds, often at over 1/1000 of a second. It's like taking sports pictures. You shoot fast and try to guess what the next action will be.

Dolphins are fast and graceful, and they can make me feel slow and awkward in the water. The best pictures are taken when they let me be part of their lives, when they go about their business, or play near me. When that happens, I get not only good pictures but also some of the most memorable moments of my life.

FOR EACH OF OUR PARENTS, WHO SHOWED US THE AMAZING NATURAL WORLD WHEN WE WERE YOUNG AND STARTED US ON OUR WAY. THANK YOU, MOMS AND DADS! —LN & FN

Acknowledgments
I am deeply grateful to the researchers who share their experience and knowledge with me and help me get close to the dolphins they study. Randall Wells (Mote Marine Lab), Denise Herzing (Wild Dolphin Project), and Dr. Steve Dawson and Dr. Liz Slooten (University of Otago) are just a few of the people that made this work possible. The guidance of the late Dr. Kenneth Norris of UC Santa Cruz, the author of "Dolphins in Crisis" in NATIONAL GEOGRAPHIC magazine, led me through the world of dolphins. I would also like to thank the people at Dolphin Quest Hawaii for their help over the years. They and others put me in the right place at the right time and helped me understand where I was.

The publisher gratefully acknowledges the assistance of Christine Kiel, K–3 Curriculum and Reading Consultant.

Book design by David M. Seager
The body text of the book is set in ITC Century. The display text is set in Knockout and Party Noid.

Published by the National Geographic Society

John M. Fahey, Jr., *President and Chief Executive Officer*

Gilbert M. Grosvenor, *Chairman of the Board*

Nina D. Hoffman, *Executive Vice President; President, Book Publishing Group*

Staff for This Book

Nancy Laties Feresten, *Vice President, Editor-in-Chief of Children's Books*

Bea Jackson, *Director of Design and Illustration, Children's Books*

Jennifer Emmett, Mary Beth Oelkers-Keegan, *Project Editors*

David M. Seager, *Art Director*

Lori Epstein, *Illustrations Editor*

Jocelyn G. Lindsay, *Researcher*

Jean Cantu, *Illustrations Specialist*

Carl Mehler, *Director of Maps*

Rebecca Baines, *Editorial Assistant*

Jennifer A. Thornton, *Managing Editor*

R. Gary Colbert, *Production Director*

Lewis R. Bassford, *Production Manager*

Vincent P. Ryan, Maryclare Tracy, Nicole Elliott, *Manufacturing Managers*

Front Cover: Face to face with a dolphin. *Front Flap:* An orca opens wide. *Back Cover:* A dolphin swims in for a closer look; Flip and Linda Nicklin smile for the camera. *Page One:* A bottlenose dolphin emerges to say hello. *Title Page:* Eye to eye with a dolphin.

Library of Congress Cataloging-in-Publication Data

Nicklin, Flip.
 Face to face with dolphins / by Flip and Linda Nicklin.
     p. cm.
 Includes bibliographical references and index.
  ISBN 978-1-4263-0141-4 (trade : alk. paper); ISBN 978-1-4263-0142-1 (library : alk. paper)
 1. Dolphins. I. Nicklin, Linda. II. Title.
QL737.C432N53 2007
599.53--dc22

                                    2006036273

Printed in China.

← *A large male orca in a peaceful moment*